DEDICATION

For Matt and Betty with love.

This edition published by Barnes and Noble Inc.,
By arrangement with PRC Publishing Ltd.

2002 Barnes and Noble Books

ISBN 0-7607-3085-7

M 10 9 8 7 6 5 4 3 2 1

Produced by PRC Publishing Ltd.
64 Brewery Road, London N7 9NT

Photographs © David Lyons 1996
Design and Layout © PRC Publishing Ltd 1996

Printed and bound in China

INTRODUCTION

In this collection I have tried to bring together examples of some of the many flavours which go to conjure the banquet which is Irish poetry, from the first written manuscripts of the bards of the ancient Celts to Yeats, the great man of our own century. And if I could invite the reader to that banquet and if all the writers gathered here in this anthology were fellow guests, what an evening we would have! Wouldn't the conversation be something grand; and after a thread or two of whiskey had combined with the curl of peat smoke we'd find ourselves in company with the finest philosophers in Europe – debating the price of a horse or the best fly for a trout in a language rich in delight. And for sure there are a few lamenting their long lost love or charming their next over a bottle of stout. Thomas More has provided a big bunch of blushing roses for them on the table and he's frowning at Percy French who has taken over the parlour with his light sparkling wit. Over in the corner there's your man singing of Saxons and patriots and 'Dark Rosaleen' and there's talk of cousins and nephews gone for Chicago or Sydney that never came back, but might, and Ossian, the old bard's tuning his harp up to the whistle and John Synge is playing the spoons he brought back from the Aran Islands.

Many years ago when I was first learning my craft as a photographer I remember coming across a portrait by the American photographer Alvin Langdon Coburn. A visitor to Dublin, he had been invited to a dinner party where the young Yeats had recited one of his recent compositions *The Song of Wandering Aengus*. Coburn persuaded him to repeat the poem in front of his camera. Coburn captured the ecstacy in the eyes of the young visionary as his words flowed. At the time I thought, as a photographer, if only I could see with those eyes.

In all the Irish poetry I have read in the preparation of this book, two impressions have been pervasive regardless of subject or period or outlook. One is the Irish writer's sheer delight in words and the weaving of stories and the other is their aching love for their land. For those who already know that delight and that love I hope this selection of words and pictures might reconfirm them. For those new to the land of the Irish poets, welcome, and I hope that you enjoy the fare.

David Lyons
Langdale, January 1996

Prelude

Still south I went and west and south again,
Through Wicklow from the morning till the night,
And far from cities, and the sights of men,
Lived with the sunshine, and the moon's delight.

I knew the stars, the flowers, and the birds,
The grey and wintry sides of many glens,
And did but half remember human words,
In converse with the mountains, moors, and fens.

J.M.Synge
1871-1909

Waxies Dargle

Says my aul' one to your aul' one
Will yeh come to the Waxies Dargle
Says your aul' one to my aul' one
Shure I haven't got a farthin'
I've just been down to Monto Town
To see young Kill McArdle
But he wouldn't lend me half a crown
To go to the Waxies Dargle

Chorus
What are you havin'
Will you have a pint
Yes I'll have a pint
With you sir
And if one of ye doesn't order soon
We'll be thrown out of the boozer

Says my aul' one to your aul' one
Will you come to the Galway Races
Says your aul' one to my aul' one

With the price of my aul' lad's braces
I went down to Capel Street
To the Jew man money lenders
But they wouldn't give me a
couple of bob on
My aul' lad's red suspenders

Chorus

Says my aul' one to your aul' one
We have no beef or mutton
But if we go down to Monto Town
We might get a drink for nuttin
Here's a piece of fine advice
I got from an aul' fishmonger
When food is scarce
And you see the hearse
You'll know you have died of hunger

Chorus

Anonymous

5

The Kine of My Father

The kine of my father, they are straying from my keeping;
    The young goat's at mischief, but little can I do:
For all through the night did I hear the banshee keening;
O youth of my loving, and is it well with you?

All through the night sat my mother with my sorrow;
    'Wisht, it is the storm, O one childeen of my heart!'
My hair with the wind, and my two hands clasped in anguish;
    Black head of my darling! too long we are apart.

Were your grave at my feet, I would think it half a blessing;
    I could herd then the cattle and drive the goats away;
Many a Paternoster I would say for your safe keeping;
    I could sleep above your heart until the dawn of day.

I see you on the prairie, hot with thirst and faint with hunger;
    The head that I love lying low upon the sand.
The vultures shriek impatient, and the coyote dogs are howling,
    Till the blood is pulsing cold within your clenching hand.

I see you on the waters, so white, so still, forsaken,
    Your dear eyes unclosing beneath a foreign rain:
A plaything of the winds, you turn and drift unceasing;
    No grave for your resting; Oh, mine the bitter pain!

All through the night did I hear the banshee keening:
    Somewhere you are dying, and nothing can I do:
My hair with the wind, and my two hands clasped in anguish;
    Bitter is my trouble – and I am far from you.

Dora Sigerson Shorter
1866-1918

A Lament

Youth's bright palace
Is overthrown,
With its diamond sceptre
And golden throne;
As a time-worn stone
Its turrets are humbled, –
All hath crumbled
But grief alone!

Whither, oh! whither
Have fled away
The dreams and hopes
Of my early day?
Ruined and grey
Are the towers I builded;
And the beams that gilded
Ah! where are they?

Once this world
Was fresh and bright,
With its golden noon
And its starry night;
Glad and light,
By mountain and river,
Have I blessed the Giver
With hushed delight.

Youth's illusions,
One by one,
Have passed like clouds
That the sun looked on.
While morning shone,
How purple their fringes!
How ashy their tinges
When that was gone!

As fire-flies fade
When the nights are damp –
As meteors are quenched
In a stagnant swamp –
Thus Charlemagnes's camp,
Where the Paladins rally,
And the Diamond Valley,
And the Wonderful Lamp

And all the wonders
Of Ganges and Nile,
And Haroun's rambles,
And Crusoe's isle,
And Princes who smile
On the Genii's daughters
'Neath the Orient waters
Full many a mile,

And all that the pen
Of Fancy can write
Must vanish
In manhoods misty light –
Squire and Knight,
And damosels' glances,
Sunny romances
So pure and bright!

These have vanished,
And what remains?
Life's budding garlands
Have turned to chains –
Its beams and rains
Feed but docks and thistles,
And sorrow whistles
O'er desert plains!

Denis Florence MacCarthy

I Am Ireland

I am Ireland:
I am older than the Old Woman of Beare.

Great my glory:
I that bore Cuchulainn the valiant.

Great my shame:
My own children that sold their mother.

I am Ireland:
I am lonelier than the Old Woman of Beare.

Patrick Pearse
1879-1916

Deidrê's Lament for the Sons of Usnach

The lions of the hill are gone,
And I am left alone–alone –
Dig the grave both wide and deep,
For I am sick, and fain would sleep!

The falcons of the wood are flown,
And I am left alone–alone –
Dig the grave both deep and wide,
And let us slumber side by side.

The dragons of the rock are sleeping,
Sleep that wakes not for our weeping –
Dig the grave, and make it ready,
Lay me on my true-love's body.

Lay their spears and bucklers bright
By the warriors' sides aright;
Many a day the three before me
On their linkèd bucklers bore me.

Lay upon the low grave floor,
'Neath each head, the blue claymore;
Many a time the noble three
Reddened their blue blades for me.

Lay the collars, as is meet,
Of the greyhounds at their feet;
Many a time for me have they
Brought the tall red deer to bay.

In the falcon's jesses throw,
Hook and arrow, line and bow;
Never again, by stream or plain,
Shall the gentle woodsmen go.

Sweet companions, were ye ever –
Harsh to me, your sister, never;
Woods and wilds, and misty valleys,
Were with you as good's a palace.

O, to hear my true-love singing,
Sweet as sounds of trumpets ringing;
Like the sway of ocean swelling
Rolled his deep voice round our dwelling.

O! to hear the echos pealing
Round our green and fairy shealing
When the three, with soaring chorus,
Passed the silent skylark o'er us

Echo now, sleep morn and even -
Lark alone enchant the heaven!
Ardan's lips are scant of breath,
Neesa's tongue is cold in death.

Stag, exult on glen and mountain –
Salmon, leap from loch to fountain –
Heron, in the free air warm ye –
Usnach's sons no more will harm ye!

Erin's stay no more you are,
Rulers of the ridge of war;
Never more 'twill be your fate
To keep the beam of battle straight.

Woe is me! by fraud and wrong,
Traitors false and tyrants strong,
Fell Clan Usnach, bought and sold,
For Barach's feast and Conor's gold!

Woe to Eman, roof and wall!
Woe to Red Branch, hearth and hall! –
Tenfold woe and black dishonour
To the foul and false Clan Conor!

Dig the grave both wide and deep,
Sick I am, and fain would sleep!
Dig the grave and make it ready,
Lay me on my true-loves's body

Samuel Ferguson
1810-1886
His translation from ancient Erse

Down by the Salley Gardens

Down by the salley gardens my love and I did meet;
She passed the salley gardens with little snow-white feet.
She bid me take love easy, as the leaves grow on the tree;
But I, being young and foolish, with her would not agree.

In a field by the river my love and I did stand,
And on my leaning shoulder she laid her snow-white hand.
She bid me take life easy, as the grass grows on the weirs;
But I was young and foolish, and now am full of tears.

W.B.Yeats
1865-1939

To the Lady of Drisheen

Lady, in your high grey house
under the ash tree
above the blue spruce,
will you spare a little of your space for me?

In your lanes wild strawberries stray
like red thoughts amongst green;
purple loosestrife takes ease here
with foxglove, fern and meadowsweet.

You call your cattle home in the evening
from the sloping field in the western sun,
on the Ilen estuary where sea-trout are flashing
their silver bellies - everyone

slipping away downriver from the stalking heron
and mouth of the fat seal.
Beyond Leap in a grey heaven
over the pikey water the curlew grieves.

Now the new moon is patterning her shining self
behind the black fret of ashleaves,
while the sun slides behind the Cork hills
down the Atlantic, out of our daylight lives.

So I am easier for knowing that you are there
in the tall house over the estuary.
Lady, I pray you always to keep open
a little of your generous space for me.

© *Anne Smith*

Do You Remember That Night?

Do you remember that night
When you were at the window
With neither hat nor gloves
Nor coat to shelter you?
I reached out my hand to you
And you ardently grasped it,
I remained to converse with you
Until the lark began to sing.

Do you remember that night
That you and I were
At the foot of the rowan-tree
And the night drifting snow?
Your head on my breast,
And your pipe sweetly playing?
Little thought I that night
That our love ties would loosen!

Beloved of my inmost heart,
Come some night, and soon,
When my people are at rest,
That we may talk together.
My arms shall encircle you
While I relate my sad tale,
That your soft, pleasent converse
Hath deprived me of heaven.

The fire is unraked,
The light unextinguished,
The key under the door,
Do you softly draw it.
My mother is asleep,
But I am wide awake;
My fortune in my hand,
I am ready to go with you.

Eugene O'Curry
1796-1862

The Song of Wandering Aengus

I went out to the hazel wood,
Because a fire was in my head,
And cut and peeled a hazel wand,
And hooked a berry to a thread;
And when white moths were on the wing,
And moth-like stars were flickering out,
I dropped the berry in a stream
And caught a little silver trout.

When I had laid it on the floor
I went to blow the fire aflame,
But something rustled on the floor,
And some one called me by my name:
It had become a glimmering girl
With apple blossom in her hair
Who called me by my name and ran
And faded through the brightening air.

Though I am old with wandering
Through hollow lands and hilly lands,
I will find out where she has gone,
And kiss her lips and take her hands;
And walk among long dappled grass,
And pluck till time and times are done
The silver apples of the moon,
The golden apples of the sun.

W.B.Yeats
1865-1939

Herring is King

Let all the fish that swim the sea,
  Salmon and turbot, cod and ling,
Bow down the head and bend the knee
  To herring, their king! to herring, their king!

    Sing, Hugamar féin and sowra lin',
    'Tis we have brought the summer in.[1]

The sun sank down so round and red
  Upon the bay, upon the bay;
The sails shook idly overhead,
  Becalmed we lay; becalmed we lay;

    Sing, Hugamar féin and sowra lin',
    'Tis we have brought the summer in.

Till Shawn the eagle dropped on deck,
  The bright-eyed boy, the bright-eyed boy;
'Tis he has spied your silver track,
  Herring, our joy, herring, our joy;

    Sing, Hugamar féin and sowra lin',
    'Tis we have brought the summer in.

It is in with the sails and away to shore,
  With the rise and swing, the rise and swing
Of two stout lads at each smoking oar,
  After herring, our king! herring, our king.

    Sing, Hugamar féin an sowra lin'
    'Ti we have brought the summer in!

The Manx and Cornish raised the shout,
  And joined the chase, and joined the chase ;
But their fleets they fouled as they went about,
  And we won the race, we won the race;

    Sing, Hugamar féin an sowra lin'
    'Tis we have brought the summer in!

For we turned and faced you full to land,
  Down the góleen[2] long, the góleen long,
And after you slipped from strand to strand
  Our nets so strong, our nets so strong;

    Sing, Hugamar féin an sowra lin'
    'Tis we have brought the summer in!

Then we called to our sweethearts and our wives,
  'Come welcome us home, welcome us home,'
Till they ran to meet us for their lives
Into the foam, into the foam;

    Sing, Hugamar féin an sowra lin'
    'Tis we have brought the summer in!

O kissing of hands and waving of caps
  From girl and boy, from girl and boy,
While you leapt by scores in the lasses' laps,
  Herring our joy, herring our joy!

    Sing, Hugamar féin an sowra lin'
    'Tis we have brought the summer in!

Alfred Percival Graves
1846-1931

1 The second line translates the first
2 Creek

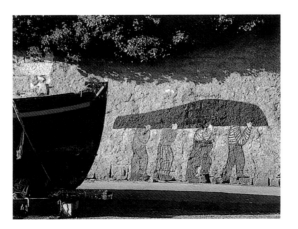

I Saw From the Beach

I saw from the beach, when the morning was shining,
   A bark o'er the waters move gloriously on;
I came when the sun from that beach was declining,
   The bark was still there, but the waters were gone.

And such is the fate of our life's early promise,
   So passing the spring-tide of joy we have known;
Each wave, that we danc'd on at morning, ebbs from us,
   And leaves us, at eve, on the bleak shore alone.

Ne'er tell me of glories, serenely adorning
   The close of our day, the calm eve of our night; –
Give me back, give me back the wild freshness of Morning,
   Her clouds and her tears are worth Evening's best light.

Thomas Moore
1779-1852

Phil the Fluther's Ball

Have you heard of Phil the Fluther, of the town of Ballymuck?
The times were going hard with him, in fact the man was bruk',
So he just sent out a notice to his neighbours, one and all,
As how he'd like their company that ev'ning at a ball.
And when writin' out he was careful to suggest to them,
That if they found a hat of his convaniant to the dure,
The more they put in, whenever he requested them,
'The better would the music be for battherin' the flure.'

Chorus
With the toot of the flute,
And the twiddle of the fiddle, O'
Hopping in the middle, like a herrin' on a griddle, O'
Up, down, hands a-rown'
Crossin' to the wall,
Oh! hadn't we the gaiety at Phil the Fluther's Ball!

There was Misther Denis Dogherty, who kep' 'The Runnin' Dog'
There was little crooked Paddy from the Tiraloughett bog:
There were boys from every Barony, and girls from every 'art,'
And the beautiful Miss Bradys, in a private ass an' cart.
And along with them came bouncing Mrs. Cafferty,
Little Micky Mulligan was also to the fore,
Rose, Suzanne, and Margaret O'Rafferty,
The flower of Ardmagullion, and the Pride of Pethravore.

Chorus

First little Micky Mulligan got up to show them how,
And then the widda' Cafferty steps out and makes her bow.
'I could dance you off your legs,' sez she, 'as sure as you are born,
If ye'll only make the piper play "the hare was in the corn".'
So, Phil plays up to the best of his ability,
The lady and the gentleman begin to do their share;
Faith, then Mick, it's you that has agility!
Begorra! Mrs. Cafferty, yer leppin' like a hare!

Chorus

Then Phil the Fluther tipped a wink to little crooked Pat,
'I think it's nearly time,' sez he, 'for passin' round the hat.'
So Paddy passed the caubeen round, and looking mighty cute,
Sez, 'Ye've got to pay the piper when he toothers on the flute.'
Then all joined in wid the greatest joviality,
Covering the buckle and the shuffle, and the cut;
Jigs were danced, of very finest quality,
But the Widda bet the company at 'handeling the fut.'

Percy French
1854-1920

I Don't Mind If I Do

Now you asked me to sing you a bit of a song,
Tis not very short and it's not very long,
You asked me to sing about something that's new,
'Be-dad, now,' says I 'I Don't mind if I do.'

Well my name 'tis Dan Murphy and a farmer am I,
I courted a lass and I felt rather shy,
She invited me in for a moment to two,
'Be-dad, now,' says I, 'I don't mind if I do.'

When we entered the kitchen it was cozy, and bright,
Soon a fine hearty supper I put out of sight,
Says she, 'Would you care for one glass or two?'
'Be-dad, now,' says I, 'I don't mind if I do.'

When the supper was finished, I reached for my hat,
Said Peggy, the darling, " don't leave me like that,
Now wouldn't you care for just one kiss or two?"
'Be-dad, now,' says I, 'I don't mind if I do.'

So we talked about that and we talked about this,
Bearing the time she was stealing a kiss,
'Do you love me?' asked Peggy, 'For I do love you'
'Be-dad now,' says I, 'I don't mind if I do.'

So we hugged and we squeezed in fond lover's delight,
Said Peggy, the darling, "Please make me your wife,
I've an acre of ground and I've one cow or two,'
'Be-dad now,' says I, 'I don't mind if I do.'

We went the next morning to the Church to be wed.
The preacher presented the book and he said,
'Now let you take Peggy and Peggy'll take you,'
'Be-dad now,' says I, 'I don't mind if I do.'

Twelve months we've been married and we've one little lad,
The neighbours do swear that he's just like his dad,
But Peggy wants more, at least one or two,
'Be-dad, now,' says I, ' I don't mind if I do.'

Anonymous

All Things Bright and Beautiful

All things bright and beautiful,
  All creatures great and small,
All things wise and wonderful,
  The Lord God made them all.

Each little flower that opens,
  Each little bird that sings,
He made their glowing colours,
  He made their tiny wings.

The purple-headed mountain,
  The river running by,
The sunset and the morning
  That brightens up the sky –

The cold wind in the winter,
  The pleasant summer sun,
The ripe fruits in the garden –
  He made them every one;

The tall trees in the greenwood,
  The meadows where we play,
The rushes by the water
  We gather every day –

He gave us eyes to see them,
  And lips that we might tell
How great is God Almighty,
  Who has made all things well.

Cecil Frances Alexander
1818-1895

Under the Round Tower

'Although I'd lie lapped up in linen
A deal I'd sweat and little earn
If I should live as live the neighbours,'
Cried the beggar, Billy Byrne;
'Stretch bones till the daylight come
On great-grandfather's battered tomb.'

Upon a grey old battered tombstone
In Glendalough beside the stream,
Where the O'Byrnes and Byrnes are buried,
He stretched his bones and fell in a dream
Of sun and moon that a good hour
Bellowed and pranced in the round tower;

Of golden king and silver lady,
Bellowing up and bellowing round,
Till toes mastered a sweet measure,
Mouth mastered a sweet sound,
Prancing round and prancing up
Until they pranced upon the top.

That golden king and that wild lady
Sang till stars began to fade,
Hands gripped in hands, toes close together,
Hair spread on the wind they made;
That lady and that golden king
Could like a brace of blackbirds sing.

'It's certain that my luck is broken,'
That rambling jailbird Billy said;
'Before nightfall I'll pick a pocket
And snug it in a feather-bed.
I cannot find the peace of home
On great-grandfather's battered tomb.'

W.B.Yeats
1865-1939

The Celts

Long, long ago, beyond the misty space
  Of twice a thousand years,
In Erin old there dwelt a mighty race,
  Taller than Roman spears;
Like oaks and towers they had a giant grace,
  Were fleet as deers,
With wind and waves they made their 'biding place,
  These western shepherd seers.

Their Ocean-God was Manannan MacLir,
  Whose angry lips,
In their white foam, full often would inter
  Whole fleets of ships;
Cromah their Day-God, and their Thunderer
  Made morning and eclipse;
Bride was their Queen of Song, and unto her
  They prayed with fire-touched lips.

Great were their deeds, their passions and their sports;
  With clay and stone
They piled on strath and shore those mystic forts,
  Not yet o'erthrown;
On cairn-crowned hills they held their council-courts;
  While youths alone,
With giant dogs, explored the elk resorts,
  And bought them down.

Of these was Finn, the father of the Bard
  Whose ancient song
Over the clamor of all change is heard,
  Sweet-voiced and strong.
Finn once o'ertook Grania, the golden-haired,
  The fleet and young;
From her the lovely, and from him the feared,
  The primal poet sprung.

Ossian! two thousand years of mist and change
  Surround thy name –
Thy Fenian heroes now no longer range
  The hills of fame.
The very names of Finn and Gaul sound strange –
  Yet thine the same –
By miscalled lake and desecrated grange –
  Remains, and shall remain!

The Druid's altar and the Druid's creed
  We scarce can trace,
There is not left an undisputed deed
  Of all your race,
Save your majestic song, which hath their speed,
  And strength and grace
In that sole song, they live and love, and bleed –
  It bears them on through space.

O, inspired giant! shall we e'er behold,
  In our own time,
One fit to speak your spirit on the wold,
  Or seize your rhyme?
One pupil of the past, as mighty-souled
  As in the prime,
Were the fond, fair, and beautiful, and bold –
  They of your song sublime!

Thomas D'Arcy McGee
1825-1868

The Harp That Once Through Tara's Halls

The harp that once through Tara's halls
    The soul of music shed,
Now hangs as mute on Tara's walls
    As if that soul were fled.
So sleeps the pride of former days,
    So glory's thrill is o'er,
And hearts that once beat high for praise,
    Now feel that pulse no more!

No more to chiefs and ladies bright
    The harp of Tara swells;
The chord alone that breaks at night,
    Its tale of ruin tells.
Thus Freedom now so seldom wakes,
    The only throb she gives
Is when some heart indignant breaks,
    To show that still she lives.

Thomas Moore
1779-1852

(Lines From) The Deserted Village

Sweet Auburn! loveliest village of the plain;
Where health and plenty cheered the laboring swain,
Where smiling spring its earliest visit paid,
And parting summer's lingering blooms delayed:
Dear lovely bowers of innocence and ease,
Seats of my youth, when every sport could please,
How often have I loitered o'er thy green,
Where humble happiness endeared each scene!
How often have I paused on every charm,
The sheltered cot, the cultivated farm,
The never-failing brook, the busy mill,
The decent church that topped the neighboring hill,
The hawthorn bush, with seats beneath the shade,
For talking age and whispering lovers made!
How often have I blest the coming day,
When toil remitting lent its turn to play,
And all the village train, from labor free,
Led up their sports beneath the spreading tree,
While many a pastime circled in the shade,
The young contending as the old surveyed;
And many a gambol frolicked o'er the ground,
And sleights of art and feats of strength went round.
And still, as each repeated pleasure tired,
Succeeding sports the mirthful band inspired;
The dancing pair that simply sought renown,
By holding out to tire each other down;
The swain mistrustless of his smutted face.
While secret laughter tittered round the place;
The bashful virgin's side-long looks of love,
The matron's glance that would those looks reprove:
These were thy charms, sweet village! sports like these,
With sweet succession, taught even toil to please:
These round thy bowers their cheerful influence shed:
These were thy charms – but all these charms are fled.
 Sweet smiling village, loveliest of the lawn,
Thy sports are fled, and all thy charms withdrawn:

Amidst thy bowers the tyrant's hand is seen,
And desolation saddens all thy green:
One only master grasps the whole domain,
And half a tillage stints thy smiling plain,
No more thy glassy brook reflects the day,
But, choked with sedges, works its weedy way;
Along thy glades a solitary guest,
The hollow sounding bittern guards its nest;
Amidst thy desert walks the lapwing flies,
And tires their echoes with unvaried cries;
Sunk are thy bowers in shapeless ruin all,
And the long grass o'er-tops the moldering wall;
And trembling, shrinking from the spoiler's hand,
Far, far away thy children leave the land.

Ill fares the land, to hastening ills a prey,
Where wealth accumulates, and men decay:
Princes and lords may flourish, or may fade;
A breath can make them, as a breath has made;
But a bold peasantry, their country's pride,
When once destroyed, can never be supplied.

. . . .

In all my wanderings round this world of care,
In all my grief – and God has given my share –
I still had hopes, my latest hours to crown,
Amidst these humble bowers to lay me down;
To husband out life's taper at the close,
And keep the flame from wasting by repose:

I still had hopes, for pride attends us still,
Amidst the swains to show my book-learned skill,
Around my fire an evening group to draw,
And tell of all I felt, and all I saw;
And, as an hare whom hounds and horns pursue,
Pants to the place from whence at first she flew,
I still had hopes, my long vexations past,
Here to return – and die at home at last.

. . . .

Sweet was the sound, when oft at evening's close
Up yonder hill the village murmur rose.
There, as I passed with careless steps and slow,
The mingling notes came softened from below;
The swain responsive as the milk-maid sung,
The sober herd that lowed to meet their young,
The noisy geese that gabbled o'er the pool,
The playful children just let loose from school,
The watch-dog's voice that bayed the whispering wind,
And the loud laugh that spoke the vacant mind; –
These all in sweet confusion sought the shade,
And filled each pause the nightingale had made.
But now the sounds of population fail,
No cheerful murmurs fluctuate in the gale,
No busy steps the grass-grown foot-way tread,
For all the bloomy flush of life is fled.

Oliver Goldsmith
c1730-1774

Dark Rosaleen

O my Dark Rosaleen,
  Do not sigh, do not weep!
The priests are on the ocean green,
  They march along the Deep.
There's wine. . . from the royal Pope
  Upon the ocean green;
And Spanish ale shall give you hope,
  My Dark Rosaleen!
  My own Rosaleen!
Shall glad your heart, shall give you hope,
Shall give you health, and help, and hope,
  My Dark Rosaleen.

Over hills and through dales
  Have I roamed for your sake;
All yesterday I sailed with sails
  On river and on lake.
The Erne. . . at its highest flood
  I dashed across unseen,
For there was lightening in my blood,
  My Dark Rosaleen!
  My own Rosaleen!
Oh! there was lightening in my blood,
Red lightning lightened through my blood,
  My Dark Rosaleen!

All day long in unrest
  To and fro do I move,
The very soul within my breast
  Is wasted for you, love!
The heart . . . in my bosom faints
  To think of you, my Queen,
My life of life, my saint of saints,
  My Dark Rosaleen!
  My own Rosaleen!
To hear your sweet and sad complaints,
My life, my love, my saint of saints,
  My Dark Rosaleen!

Woe and pain, pain and woe,
   Are my lot night and noon,
To see your bright face clouded so,
   Like to the mournful moon.
But yet . . .will I rear your throne
   Again in golden sheen;
'Tis you shall reign, shall reign alone,
   My Dark Rosaleen!
   My own Rosaleen!
'Tis you shall have the golden throne,
'Tis you shall reign, and reign alone,
   My Dark Rosaleen!

Over dews, over sands
   Will I fly for your weal;
Your holy delicate white hands
   Shall girdle me with steel.
At home . . .in your emerald bowers,
   From morning's dawn till e'en,
You'll pray for me, my flower of flowers,
   My Dark Rosaleen!
   My fond Rosaleen!
You'll think of me through Daylight's hours,
My virgin flower, my flower of flowers,
   My Dark Rosaleen!

I could scale the blue air,
   I could plough the high hills,
Oh, I could kneel all night in prayer,
   To heal your many ills!
And one . . . beamy smile from you
   Would float like light between
My toils and me, my own, my true,
   My Dark Rosaleen!
   My fond Rosaleen!
Would give me life and soul anew,
A second life, a soul anew,
   My Dark Rosaleen!

O! the Erne shall run red
   With redundance of blood,
The earth shall rock beneath our tread,
   And flames wrap hill and wood,
And gun-peal, and slogan cry,
   Wake many a glen serene,
Ere you shall fade, ere you shall die,
   My Dark Rosaleen!
   My own Rosaleen!
The Judgement Hour must first be nigh,
Ere you can fade, ere you can die,
   My Dark Rosaleen!

James Clarence Mangan
1803-1849

An Irish Airman Forsees His Death

I know that I shall meet my fate
Somewhere among the clouds above;
Those that I fight I do not hate,
Those that I guard I do not love;
My country is Kiltartan Cross,
My countrymen Kiltartan's poor,
No likely end could bring them loss
Or leave them happier than before.
Nor law, nor duty bade me fight,
Nor public men, nor cheering crowds,
A lonely impulse of delight
Drove to this tumult in the clouds;
I balanced all, brought all to mind,
The years to come seemed waste of breath,
A waste of breath the years behind
In balance with this life, this death.

W.B.Yeats
1865-1939

The Minstrel Boy

The Minstrel Boy to the war is gone,
In the ranks of the dead you'll find him;
His father's sword he has girded on,
And his wild harp slung behind him.
'Land of song', said the warrior bard,
'Though all the world betray thee,
One sword, at least, thy rights shall guard,
One faithful harp shall praise thee.'

The Minstrel fell – but the foeman's chain
Could not bring his proud soul under;
The harp he lov'd ne'er spoke again,
For he tore its chords asunder;
And said, 'No chains shall sully thee,
Thou soul of love and bravery.
Thy songs were made for the pure and free,
They shall never sound in slavery.'

Thomas Moore
1779-1852

The Madness of King Goll

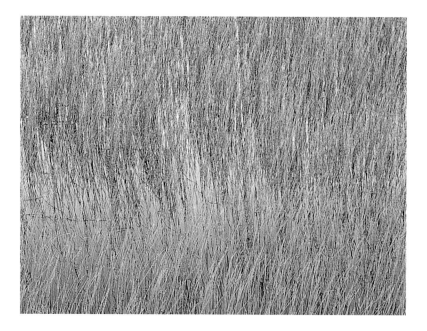

I sat on cushioned otter skin:
My word was law from Ith to Eman,
And shook at Invar Amargin
The hearts of the world-troubling seamen,
And drove tumult and war away
From girl and boy and man and beast;
The fields grew fatter day by day,
The wild fowl of the air increased;
And every ancient Ollave said,
While he bent down his fading head,
'He drives away the Northern cold.'
They will not hush, the leaves a-flutter round me,
the beech leaves old.

I sat and mused and drank sweet wine;
A herdsman came from inland valleys,
Crying, the pirates drove his swine
To fill their dark-beaked hollow galleys.
I called my battle-breaking men,
And my loud brazen battle-cars
From rolling vale and rivery glen;
And under the blinking of the stars
Fell on the pirates by the deep,
And hurled them in the gulph of sleep:
These hands won many a torque of gold.
They will not hush, the leaves a-flutter round me,
the beech leaves old.

But slowly, as I shouting slew
And trampled in the bubbling mire,
In my most secret spirit grew
A whirling and a wandering fire:
I stood: keen stars above me shone,
Around me shone keen eyes of men:
I laughed aloud and hurried on
By rocky shore and rushy fen;
I laughed because birds fluttered by,
And starlight gleamed, and clouds flew high,
And rushes waved and waters rolled.
They will not hush, the leaves a-flutter round me,
the beech leaves old.

And now I wander in the woods
When summer gluts the golden bees,
Or in autumnal solitudes
Arise the leopard-colored trees;
Or when along the wintry strands
The cormorants shiver on their rocks;
I wander on, and wave my hands,
And sing, and shake my heavy locks.
The gray wolf knows me; by one ear
I lead along the woodland deer;
The hares run by me growing bold.
They will not hush, the leaves a-flutter round me,
the beech leaves old.

I came upon a little town,
That slumbered in the harvest moon,
And passed a-tiptoe up and down,
Murmuring, to a fitful tune,
How I have followed, night and day,
A tramping of tremendous feet,
And saw where this old tympan lay,
Deserted on a doorway seat,
And bore it to the woods with me;
Of some unhuman misery
Our married voices wildly trolled.
They will not hush, the leaves a-flutter round me,
the beech leaves old.

I sang how, when day's toil is done,
Orchil shakes out her long dark hair
That hides away the dying sun
And sheds faint odors through the air:
When my hand passed from wire to wire
It quenched, with sound like falling dew,
The whirling and the wandering fire;
But lift a mournful ulalu,
For the kind wires are torn and still,
And I must wander wood and hill
Through summer's heat and winter's cold.
They will not hush, the leaves a-flutter round me,
the beech leaves old.

W.B.Yeats
1865-1939

The Lake Isle of Innisfree

I will arise and go now, and go to Innisfree,
   And a small cabin build there, of clay and wattles made;
Nine bean rows will I have there, a hive for the honey bee,
   And live alone in the bee-loud glade.

And I shall have some peace there, for peace comes dropping slow,
   Dropping from the veils of the morning to where the cricket sings;
There midnight's all a glimmer, and noon a purple glow,
   And evening full of the linnet's wings.

I will arise and go now, for always night and day
   I hear lake water lapping with low sounds by the shore;
While I stand on the roadway, or on the pavements gray,
   I hear it in the deep heart's core.

W.B.Yeats
1865-1939

Running To Paradise

As I came over Windy Gap
They threw a halfpenny into my cap,
For I am running to Paradise;
And all that I need do is to wish
And somebody puts his hand in the dish
To throw me a bit of salted fish:
And *there the king is but as the beggar*

My Brother Mourteen is worn out
With skelping his big brawling lout,
And I am running to Paradise;
A poor life, do what he can,
And though he keep a dog and a gun,
A serving-maid and a serving-man:
And *there the king is but as the beggar.*

Poor men have grown to be rich men,
And rich men grown to be poor again,
And I am running to Paradise;
And many a darling wit's grown dull
That tossed a bare heel when at school,
Now it has filled an old sock full:
And *there the king is but as the beggar.*

The wind is old and still at play
While I must hurry upon my way,
For I am running to Paradise;
Yet never have I lit on a friend
To take my fancy like the wind
That nobody can buy or bind:
And *there the king is but as the beggar.*

W.B.Yeats
1865-1939

The Mystery of Amergin

I am the wind which breathes upon the sea,
I am the wave of the ocean,
I am the murmur of the billows,
I am the ox of the seven combats,
I am the vulture upon the rocks,
I am a beam of the sun,
I am the fairest of plants,
I am a wild boar in valour,
I am a salmon in the water,
I am a lake in the plain.
I am a word of science,
I am the point of the lance of battle,

I am the God who creates in the head the fire
Who is it who throws light into the meeting on the mountain?
Who announces the ages of the moon [If not I]?
Who teaches the place where couches the sun [If not I]?

Ancient Erse

The Dark Man

Rose o' the world, she came to my bed
And changed the dreams of my heart and head :
For joy of mine she left grief of hers
And garlanded me with the prickly furze.

Rose o' the world, they go out and in,
And watch me dream and my mother spin:
And they pity the tears on my sleeping face
While my soul's away in a fairy place.

Rose o' the world, they have words galore,
For wide's the swing of my mother's door:
And soft they speak of my darkened brain,
But what do they know of my heart's dear pain?

Rose o' the world, the grief you give
Is worth all days that a man may live :
Is worth all prayers that the colleens say
On the night that darkens the wedding-day.

Rose o' the world, what man would wed
When he might remember your face instead ?
Might go to his grave with the blessed pain
Of hungering after your face again ?

Rose o' the world, they may talk their fill,
But dreams are good, and my life stands still
While the neighbours talk by their fires astir :
But my fiddle knows: and I talk to her.

Nora Hopper

Sea Wrack

The wrack was dark an' shiny where it floated in the sea,
There was no one in the brown boat but only him an' me;
Him to cut the sea wrack, me to mind the boat,
An' not a word between us the hours we were afloat.

    The wet wrack,

    The sea wrack,

    The wrack was strong to cut.

We laid it on the gray rocks to wither in the sun,
An' what should call my lad then, to sail from Cushendun?
With a low moon, a full tide, a swell upon the deep,
Him to sail the old boat, me to fall asleep.

    The dry wrack,

    The sea wrack,

    The wrack was dead so soon.

There' a fire low upon the rocks to burn the wrack to kelp,
There' a boat gone down upon the Moyle, an' sorra one to help!
Him beneath the salt sea, me upon the shore,
By sunlight or moonlight we'll lift the wrack no more.

    The dark wrack,

    The sea wrack,

    The wrack may drift ashore.

Moira O'Neill

The Apples Ripen Under Yellowing Leaves

The apples ripen under yellowing leaves,
And in the farm yards by the little bay
The shadows come and go amid the sheaves,
And on the long dry inland winding way:
Where, in the thinning boughs each air bereaves,
Faint sunlights golden, and the spider weaves.
Grey are the low-laid sleepy hills, and grey
The autumn solitude of the sea day,
Where from the deep 'mid-channel, less and less
You hear along the pale east afternoon
 A sound, uncertain as the silence, swoon –
The tide's sad voice ebbing toward loneliness:
And past the sands and seas' blue level line,
Ceaseless, the faint far murmur of the brine.

Thomas Caulfield Irwin
1823-1892

On Behalf of Some Irishmen Not Followers of Tradition

They call us aliens, we are told,
Because our wayward visions stray
From that dim banner they unfold,
The dreams of worn-out yesterday.
The sum of all the past is theirs,
The creeds, the deeds, the fame, the name,
Whose death-created glory flares
And dims the spark of living flame.
They weave the necromancer's spell,
And burst the graves where martyrs slept,
Their ancient story to retell,
Renewing tears the dead have wept.
And they would have us join their dirge,
This worship of an extinct fire
In which they drift beyond the verge
Where races all outworn expire.
The worship of the dead is not
A worship that our hearts allow,
Though every famous shade were wrought
With woven thorns above the brow.
We fling our answer back in scorn:
'We are less children of this clime
Than of some nation yet unborn
Or empire in the womb of time.
We hold the Ireland in the heart
More than the land our eyes have seen,
And love the goal for which we start
More than the tale of what has been.'

The generations as they rise
May live the life men lived before,
Still hold the thought once held as wise,
Go in and out by the same door.
We leave the easy peace it brings:
The few we are shall still unite
In fealty to unseen kings
Or unimaginable light.
We would no Irish sign efface,
But yet our lips would gladlier hail
The firstborn of the Coming Race
Than the last splendour of the Gael.
No blazoned banner we unfold -
One charge alone we give to youth,
Against the sceptred myth to hold
The golden heresy of truth.

George Russell ('AE')
1867-1935

Ireland

'Twas the dream of a God,
    And the mould of His hand,
That you shook 'neath His stroke,
    That you trembled and broke
To this beautiful land.

Here He loosed from His hold
    A brown tumult of wings,
Till the wind on the sea
    Bore the strange melody
Of an island that sings.

He made you all fair,
    You in purple and gold,
You in silver and green,
    Till no eye that has seen
Without love can behold.

I have left you behind
    In the path of the past,
With the white breath of flowers,
    With the best of God's hours,
I have left you at last.

Dora Sigerson
1866-1918

The Stolen Child

Where dips the rocky highland
   Of Sleuth Wood in the lake,
There lies a leafy island
   Where flapping herons wake
The drowsy water-rats.
There we've hid our fairy vats
Full of berries,
And of reddest stolen cherries.
Come away, O, human child!
To the woods and waters wild
With a fairy hand in hand,
For the world's more full of weeping than you can understand.

Where the wave of moonlight glosses
   The dim grey sands with light,
Far off by farthest Rosses
   We foot it all the night,
Weaving olden dances,
Mingling hands, and mingling glances,
   Till the moon has taken flight;

To and fro we leap,
   And chase the frothy bubbles,
   While the world is full of troubles.
And is anxious in its sleep.
Come away! O, human child!
To the woods and waters wild,
With a fairy hand in hand,
For the world's more full of weeping than you can understand.

Where the wandering water gushes
   From the hills above Glen-Car,
In pools among the rushes,
   That scarce could bathe a star,
We seek for slumbering trout,
   And whispering in their ears;
      We give them evil dreams,
Leaning softly out
   From ferns that drop their tears
      Of dew on the young streams.
Come! O, human child!
To the woods and waters wild,
With a fairy hand in hand,
For the world's more full of weeping than you can understand.

Away with us, he's going,
　　The solemn-eyed;
He'll hear no more the lowing
　　Of the calves on the warm hill-side.
Or the kettle on the hob
　　Sing peace into his breast;
Or see the brown mice bob
　　Round and round the oatmeal chest.
For he comes, the human child,
To the woods and waters wild,
With a fairy hand in hand,
For the world's more full of weeping than he can understand.

W.B. Yeats
1865-1939

The Northern Coast

The fields of home for me as a child were the dairy pastures of an Irish farm. A river of salmon and trout ran to the north and my window looked north over the whiskey distillery of Bushmills to the stepped headlands of the Giant's Causeway and beyond to the grey Atlantic. On still September evenings the river mist filled the valley above the church and carried the tumble of water from where a mill race turned a wheel. In the old tongue the river name meant 'the stream of the bursting torrents'. On its banks dwelt the poet Amergin, favourite of the high kings of Ireland, who sang of heroes and listened to the salmon.

These small things I learned as a child.

On sharp winter nights I had my father's work tending cattle in must-sweet byres. Barley straw for bedding. (Some of the neighbours grew barley for the distillery. Some, more mindful of mortal sin, thought that wasn't right.) Outside, the cold constellations astride the vast sky held me in thrall.

One winter a neighbour's tractor wheel split the capstone of a buried cist. A grave untended for 3,000 years opened to the sky. My grandfather led me to where rings of ancient trees hid neglected dolmens twenty times as old as the trees.

At school they taught us victors' names and dates, the profits of empires in tonnes of bananas, and the dry balancing of mathematical equations empty on either side. A mile down the road from

the classroom, the seamen's cottages lined the shore. They were strangers who talked with foreign-sounding words like 'glashen' and 'gurnet'. Farmers eat salt fish no more than fishermen gather potatoes. Two miles from the sea, I never learned to swim, but I could stand for hours in the dark theatre of sea cliffs watching the grey swell breathing under a heavy moon.

I asked my teacher why the sea was blue. She told me it reflected the sky. I asked her why the sky is blue. I think I first left my home and my fields to find out why the sky was blue.

In all our lives we grow to recognise ourselves more certainly year by year. We learn what simple things give us pleasure and how their absence leads to illness, pain or anger. Our forefathers, neighbour by neighbour, also knew these simple things, the essentials of contentment, knew them through necessity for without them they quite literally could not live. They understood their seasons, they understood their soils, their crops, and they understood that their lives were inseparably connected with them. Their own daily lives were made their songs, and their dances weaved through harvest sheaves where young-blood feuds and romances were encompassed within a village hall. Their first ancestors marked the spoor of deer they hunted and knew the woodland glades where elderberry, blackberry and hazelnuts grew, and measured the days until each returned in their different seasons. In the memories of our own families often our lives have been lived in different fields again where the soil has been hidden by concrete and we have measured our days and sold them by the hours of a factory clock.

Now, from my window, on the steady land the plough returns each time to the headrig and turns. Shallow scratches approved by their straightness each harvest erased with cutting bars and threshers with the sweet smell of tea in the tin can. Bleak runnels in cold November rain seep to sheughs that swell and flood the river meadows. The people of this place, we dip our mills in the river and grind from the stone what we can. Running up the headland the blast from the dangerous sea holds me braced above the cliff while below the edge of the vast ocean plunders the basalt rock. Between the black cliffs and the white cliffs, the glorious, plunging waves drown the wails of Cuchulainn over his slain son, dead by his own red hand; drown the saintly prayers of Patrick on high Dunseverick's rock; drown the splintering of the Armada treasure on the black dykes of Port na Spaniagh; drown the shrieks from grand Dunluce as the banqueting hall slides below the air; drown the cries from Casement's soul, still lost in Murlough Bay; drown the rantings and ravings and the bullet cracks and all giants and the little men are tangled, thrashed upon the shore. And as I count toward the seventh wave the quiet deep salmon move home across the cold Atlantic toward the mouth of the River Bush and, amongst the fields we know, four white swans alight on the water meadow and we wait for them to sing.

© David Lyons

Under the Moon

I have no happiness in dreaming of Brycelinde,
Nor Avalon the grass-green hollow, nor Joyous Isle,
Where one found Lancelot crazed and hid him for a while;
Nor Ulad, when Naoise had thrown a sail upon the wind;
Nor lands that seem too dim to be burdens on the heart:
Land-under-Wave, where out of the moon's light and the sun's
Seven old sisters wind the threads of the long-lived ones,
Land-of-the-Tower, where Aengus has thrown the gates apart,
And Wood-of-Wonders, where one kills an ox at dawn,
To find it when night falls laid on a golden bier.
Therein are many queens like Branwen and Guinevere;
And Niamh and Laban and Fand, who could change to an otter or fawn,
And the wood-woman, whose lover was changed to a blue-eyed hawk;
And whether I go in my dreams by woodland, or dun, or shore,
Or on the unpeopled waves with kings to pull at the oar,
I hear the harp-string praise them, or hear their mournful talk.
Because of something told under the famished horn
Of the hunter's moon, that hung between the night and the day,
To dream of women whose beauty was folded in dismay,
Even in an old story, is a burden not to be borne.

W.B.Yeats
1865-1939

The Host of the Air

O'Driscoll drove with a song
The wild duck and the drake
From the tall and the tufted reeds
Of the drear Hart Lake.

And he saw how the reeds grew dark
At the coming of night-tide,
And dreamed of the long dim hair
Of Bridget his bride.

He heard while he sang and dreamed
A piper piping away,
And never was piping so sad,
And never was piping so gay.

And he saw young men and young girls
Who danced on a level place,
And Bridget his bride among them,
With a sad and a gay face.

The dancers crowded about him
And many a sweet thing said,
And a young man brought him red wine
And a young girl white bread.

But Bridget drew him by the sleeve
Away from the merry bands,
To old men playing at cards
With a twinkling of ancient hands.

The bread and the wine had a doom,
For these were the host of the air;
He sat and played in a dream
Of her long dim hair.

He played with the merry old men
And thought not of evil chance,
Until one bore Bridget his bride
Away from the merry dance.

He bore her away in his arms,
The handsomest young man there,
And his neck and his breast and his arms
Were drowned in her long dim hair.

O'Driscoll scattered the cards
And out of his dream awoke:
Old men and young men and young girls
Were gone like a drifting smoke;

But he heard high up in the air
A piper piping away,
And never was piping so sad,
And never was piping so gay.

W.B.Yeats
1865-1939

The Fairy Thorn (an Ulster Ballad)

'Get up, our Anna dear, from the weary spinning-wheel;
　For your father's on the hill, and your mother is asleep:
Come up above the crags, and we'll dance a highland reel
　Around the fairy thorn on the steep.'

At Anna Grace's door 'twas thus the maidens cried,
　Three merry maidens fair in kirtles of the green;
And Anna laid the rock and the weary wheel aside,
　The fairest of the four, I ween.

They're glancing through the glimmer of the quiet eve,
　Away in milky wavings of neck and ankle bare;
The heavy-sliding stream in its sleepy song they leave,
　And the crags in the ghostly air:

And linking hand and hand, and singing as they go,
　The maids along the hill-side have ta'en their fearless way,
Till they come to where the rowan trees in lonely beauty grow
　Beside the Fairy Hawthorn grey.

The Hawthorn stands between the ashes tall and slim,
  Like matron with her twin grand-daughters at her knee;
The rowan berries cluster o'er her low head grey and dim
  In ruddy kisses sweet to see.

The merry maidens four have ranged them in a row,
  Between each lovely couple a stately rowan stem,
And away in mazes wavy, like skimming birds they go,
  Oh, never caroll'd bird like them!

But solemn is the silence of the silvery haze
  That drinks away their voices in echoless repose,
And dreamily the evening has still'd the haunted braes,
  And dreamier the gloaming grows.

And sinking one by one, like lark-notes from the sky
  When the falcon's shadow saileth across the open shaw,
Are hush'd the maidens' voices, as cowering down they lie
  In the flutter of their sudden awe.

For, from the air above, and the grassy ground beneath,
  And from the mountain-ashes and the old whitethorn between,
A Power of faint enchantment doth through their beings breathe,
  And they sink down together on the green.

They sink together silent, and stealing side to side,
  They fling their lovely arms o'er their drooping necks so fair,
Then vainly strive again their naked arms to hide,
  For their shrinking necks again are bare.

Thus clasp'd and prostrate all, with their heads together bow'd,
    Soft o'er their bosoms' beating – the only human sound –
They hear the silky footsteps of the silent fairy crowd,
    Like a river in the air, gliding round.

No scream can any raise, nor prayer can any say,
    But wild, wild, the terror of the speechless three –
For they feel fair Anna Grace drawn silently away,
    By whom they dare not look to see.

They feel their tresses twine with her parting locks of gold,
    And the curls elastic falling, as her head withdraws;
They feel her sliding arms from their tranced arms unfold,
    But they may not look to see the cause:

For heavy on their senses the faint enchantment lies
    Through all that night of anguish and perilous amaze;
And neither fear nor wonder can ope their quivering eyes
    Or their limbs from the cold ground raise,

Till out of night the earth has roll'd her dewy side,
    With every haunted mountain and streamy vale below;
When, as the mist dissolves in the yellow morning tide,
    The maidens' trance dissolveth so.

Then fly the ghastly three as swiftly as they may,
    And tell their tale of sorrow to anxious friends in vain –
They pined away and died within the year and day,
    And ne'er was Anna Grace seen again.

Samuel Ferguson
1810-1886

The Rising of the Moon A.D.1798

'Oh! then tell me, Shawn O'Ferrall,
  Tell me why you hurry so?'
'Hush, ma bouchal, hush and listen,'
  And his cheeks were all a-glow.
'I bear ordhers from the captain,
  Get you ready quick and soon,
For the pikes must be together
  At the risin' of the moon.'

'Oh! then tell me, Shawn O'Ferrall
  Where the gatherin' is to be?'
'In the ould spot by the river,
  Right well known to you and me.
One word more - for signal token
  Whistle up the marching tune,
With your pike upon your shoulder
  By the risin' of the moon.'

Out from many a mud-wall cabin
  Eyes were watching thro' that night,
Many a manly chest was throbbing
  For the blessed warning light.
Murmurs passed along the valleys
  Like the banshee's lonely croon,
And a thousand blades were flashing
  At the risin' of the moon.

There beside the singing river
  That dark mass of men was seen,
Far above the shining weapons
  Hung their own beloved green.
'Death to every foe and traitor!
  Forward! strike the marchin' tune,
And hurrah, my boys, for freedom!
  'Tis the risin' of the moon.'

Well they fought for poor old Ireland
  And full bitter was their fate
(Oh! what glorious pride and sorrow
  Fill the name of Ninety-Eight.)
Yet, thank God, e'en still are beating
  Hearts in manhood's burning noon,
Who would follow in their footsteps
  At the risin' of the moon!

John Keegan Casey
1846-1870

Cuchullin in his Chariot

'What is the cause of thy journey or thy story?'

The cause of my journey and my story
The men of Erin, yonder, as we see them,
Coming towards you on the plain.
The chariot on which is the fold, figured and cerulean,
Which is made strongly, handy, solid;
Where were active, and where were vigorous;
And where were full-wise, the noble hearted folk;
In the prolific, faithful city; –
Fine, hard, stone-bedecked, well-shafted;
Four large-chested horses in that splendid chariot;
Comely, frolicsome.

'What do we see in that chariot?'

The white-bellied, white-haired, small-eared,
Thin-sided, thin-hoofed, horse-large, steed-large horses;
With fine, shining, polished bridles;
Like a gem; or like red sparkling fire; –
Like the motion of a fawn, wounded;
Like the rustling of a loud wind in winter; –
Coming to you in that chariot. –

'What do we see in that chariot?'

We see in that chariot,
The strong, broad-chested, nimble, gray horses, –
So mighty, so broad-chested, so fleet, so choice; –
Which would wrench the sea skerries from the rocks. –
The lively, shielded, powerful horses; –
So mettlesome, so active, so clear-shining; –
Like the talon of an eagle 'gainst a fierce beast;
Which are called the beautiful Large-Gray –
The fond, large Meactroigh.

'What do we see in that chariot?'

We see in that chariot,
The horses; which are white-headed, white-hoofed, slender-legged,
Fine-haired, sturdy, imperious;
Satin-bannered, wide chested;
Small-aged, small-haired, small-eared;
Large-hearted, large-shaped, large-nostriled;
Slender-waisted, long-bodied, – and they are foal-like;
Handsome, playful, brilliant, wild-leaping;
Which are called the Dubh-Seimhlinn.

'Who sits in that chariot?'

He who sits in that chariot,
Is the warrior, able, powerful, well-worded,
Polished, brilliant, very graceful. –
There are seven sights on his eye;
And we think that that is good vision to him;
There are six bony, fat fingers,
On each hand that comes from his shoulder;
There are seven kinds of fair hair on his head; –
Brown hair next his head's skin,
And smooth red hair over that;
And fair-yellow hair, of the colour of gold;
And clasps on the top, holding it fast; –
Whose name is Cuchullin, Seimh-suailte,
Son of Aodh, son of Agh, son of other Aodh. –
His face is like red sparkles; –
Fast-moving on the plain like mountain fleet-mist;
Or like the speed of a hill hind;
Or like a hare on rented level ground. –
It was a frequent step – a fast step – a joyful step; –
The horses coming towards us:
Like snow hewing the slopes; –
The panting and the snorting,
Of the horses coming towards thee.

Ancient Erse

The Fiddler of Dooney

When I play on my fiddle in Dooney,
Folk dance like a wave of the sea;
My cousin is priest in Kilvarnet,
My brother in Mocharabuiee.

I passed my brother and cousin:
They read in their books of prayer;
I read in my book of songs
I bought at the Sligo fair.

When we come at the end of time
To Peter sitting in state,
He will smile on the three old spirits,
But call me first through the gate;

For the good are always the merry,
Save by an evil chance,
And the merry love the fiddle,
And the merry love to dance:

And when the folk there spy me,
They will all come up to me,
With 'Here is the fiddler of Dooney!'
And dance like a wave of the sea.

W.B.Yeats
1865-1939

Columcille Cecenit

O, Son of my God, what a pride, what a pleasure
    To plough the blue sea!
The waves of the fountain of deluge to measure
    Dear Eiré to thee.

We are rounding Moy-n-Olurg, we sweep by its head, and
    We plunge through Loch Foyle,
Whose swans could enchant with their music the dead, and
    Make pleasure of toil.

The host of the gulls come with joyous commotion
    And screaming and sport,
I welcome my own 'Dewy-Red' * from the ocean
    Arriving in port.

O Eiré, were wealth my desire, what a wealth were
    To gain far from thee,
In the land of the stranger, but there even health were
    A sickness to me!

Alas for the voyage O high King of Heaven
    Enjoined upon me,
For that I on the red plain of bloody Cooldrevin
    Was present to see.

How happy the son is of Dima ; no sorrow
    For him is designed,
He is having, this hour, round his own hill in Durrow
    The wish of his mind.

The sounds of the winds in the elms, like the strings of
    A harp being played,
The note of the blackbird that claps with the wings of
    Delight in the glade.

With him in Ros-Grencha the cattle are lowing
    At earliest dawn,
On the brink of the summer the pigeons are cooing
    And doves in the lawn

Three things am I leaving behind me, the very
    Most dear that I know,
Tir-Leedach I'm leaving, and Durrow and Derry,
    Alas I must go!

Yet my visit and feasting with Comgall have eased me
    At Cainneach's right hand,
All but thy government, Eiré, has pleased me,
    Thou waterfall land.

* Dearg-dreúchtach, 'Dewy-Red' - was the name
of St Columba's boat.

St Columcille

Horses With Red Umbrellas

Last Friday the night of hurricane
wind in the chimney
turned us around,
roused up the grey-haired poet
to craziness, so that a most strange quest,
a perverse task,
he set us:
'Find for me', shouting across the wind,
'show me, when we come together the next time,
horses with red umbrellas'.

'Now – where are they indeed?' I asked myself.
I have looked for them all yesterday in this town
saw alone the long descendants of the old high-kings
as they walked to and fro in the streets,
heard music of drums and shawms.
There was a man with melancholy eyes,
in a wild grassy garden,
with a mandolin, which he fingered gently,
and put away into its beautiful leather case,
but would not play.

There was a green seastone, like a door,
nothing behind it. And at six this morning,
as the thrush began,
the horses came. I saw them
all pure white in the brilliant light,
galloping down the road.
On their backs sat strong intent women
their faces aglow under the scarlet umbrellas.
I watched them, long and long, and saw
that they reached the shore

and, as witches do the unbroken eggshells,
they inverted the umbrellas for boats
and floated away over the peacock sea,
until, in the evening light,
they came to that lean ness like a finger
the lighthouse called The Big One
at the far end – but did not stay –
after floating weary miles,
came to be drowned in the nets that lie drifting
just below the surface over Atlantis.

© *Anne Smith*

By the Margin of the Great Deep

When the breath of twilight blows to flame the misty skies,
All its vaporous sapphire, violet glow and silver gleam,
With their magic flood me through the gateway of the eyes;
    I am one with the twilight's dream.

When the trees and skies and fields are one in dusky mood,
Every heart of man is rapt within the mother's breast:
Full of peace and sleep and dreams in the vasty quietude,
    I am one with their hearts at rest.

From our immemorial joys of hearth and home and love
Strayed away along the margin of the unknown tide,
All its reach of soundless calm can thrill me far above
    Word or touch from the lips beside.

Aye, and deep and deep and deeper let me drink and draw
From the olden fountain more than light or peace or dream,
Such primeval being as o'erfills the heart with awe,
    Growing one with its silent stream.

George Russell ('AE')
1867-1935

The Fair Hills of Ireland

A plenteous place is Ireland for hospitable cheer,
    Uileacan dubh O!
Where the wholesome fruit is bursting from the yellow barley ear;
    Uileacan dubh O!
There is honey in the trees where her misty vales expand,
And her forest paths, in summer, are by falling waters fann'd,
There is dew at high noontide there, and springs i'the yellow sand,
On the fair hills of holy Ireland.

Curl'd he is and ringletted, and plaited to the knee,
    Uileacan dubh O!
Each captain who comes sailing across the Irish sea;
    Uileacan dubh O!
And I will make my journey, if life and health but stand,
Unto that pleasant country, that fresh and fragrant strand,
And leave your boasted braveries, your wealth and high command,
For the fair hills of holy Ireland.

Large and profitable are the stacks upon the ground,
    Uileacan dubh O!
The butter and the cream do wondrously abound,
    Uileacan dubh O!
The cresses on the water and the sorrels are at hand,
And the cuckoo's calling daily his note of mimic bland,
And the bold thrush sings so bravely his song i'the forests grand,
On the fair hills of holy Ireland.

Samuel Ferguson
1810-1886
(Old Irish Song)

Ossian Sang

Sweet is the voice in the land of gold,
   And sweeter the music of birds that soar,
When the cry of the heron is heard on the wold,
   And the waves break softly on Bundatrore.

Down floats on the murmuring of the breeze
   The call of the cuckoo from Cossahun,
The blackbird is warbling among the trees,
   And soft is the kiss of the warming sun.

The cry of the eagle of Assaroe
   O'er the court of Mac Morne to me is sweet,
And sweet is the cry of the bird below
   Where the wave and the wind and the tall cliff meet.

Finn mac Cool is the father of me,
   Whom seven battalions of Fenians fear:
When he launches his hounds on the open lea
   Grand is their cry as they rouse the deer.

Old Gaelic

The White Birds

I would that we were, my beloved, white birds on the foam of the sea,
We tire of the flame of the meteor, before it can pass by and flee;
And the flame of the blue star of twilight, hung low on the rim of the sky,
Has awaked in our hearts, my beloved, a sadness that never may die.

A weariness comes from those dreamers, dew dabbled, the lily and rose,
Ah, dream not of them, my beloved, the flame of the meteor that goes,
Or the flame of the blue star that lingers hung low in the fall of the dew:
For I would we were changed to white birds on the wandering foam – I and you.

I am haunted by numberless islands, and many a Danaan shore,
Where Time would surely forget us, and Sorrow come near us no more,
Soon far from the rose and the lily, and the fret of the flames would we be,
Were we only white birds, my beloved, buoyed out on the foam of the sea.

W.B. Yeats
1865-1939

The Death-Song of Ossian

Such were the words of the bards in the days of song;
when the king heard the music of harps, the tales of other
times! The chiefs gathered from all their hills, and heard
the lovely sound. They praised the Voice of Cona! The
first among a thousand bards! But age is now on my
tongue ; my soul has failed! I hear, at times, the ghosts of
the bards, and learn their pleasant song. But memory fails
on my mind. I hear the call of years! They say, as they pass
along, why does Ossian sing? Soon shall he lie in the
narrow house, and no bard shall raise his fame! Roll on, ye
dark-brown years ; ye bring no joy on your course! Let the
tomb open to Ossian, for his strength has failed. The sons
of song are gone to rest. My voice remains, like a blast,
that roars, lonely, on a sea-surrounded rock, after the
winds are laid. The dark moss whistles there; the distant
mariner sees the waving trees!

Ossian
Old Gaelic

Ode

We are the music-makers
And we are the dreamers of dreams,
Wandering by lone sea-breakers,
And sitting by desolate streams; –
World-losers and world-forsakers,
On whom the pale moon gleams:
Yet we are the movers and shakers
Of the world for ever, it seems.

With wonderful deathless ditties
We build up the world's great cities,
And out of a fabulous story
We fashion an empire's glory:
One man with a dream, at pleasure,
Shall go forth and conquer a crown;
And three with a new song's measure
Can trample an empire down.

We, in the ages lying
In the buried past of the earth
Built Nineveh with our sighing,
And Babel itself with our mirth;
And o'erthrew them with prophesying,
To the old of the new world's worth;
For each age is a dream that is dying,
Or one that is coming to birth

Arthur O'Shaughnessy
1844-1881